Highlights

The Highlights Book of
Things to Do
INDOORS

HIGHLIGHTS PRESS
HONESDALE, PENNSYLVANIA

CONTENTS

3 How to Use This Book

4 All About You

24 Fun and Games

44 Amazing Adventures

62 Go Wild

82 Boost Your Brain

102 Helping Others

122 Supercool Science

142 Reuse It!

158 Answer Key

160 Credits

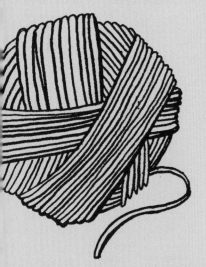

HOW TO USE THIS BOOK

It's completely up to you how you use this book. You can start at the beginning or flip to the end and work backward. Or you can jump around to all the pages that spark your interest. You can also complete the activities based on how you're feeling. If you're feeling energetic, you might choose to flip to the chapter called "Amazing Adventures." If you love animals, you can get started in the "Go Wild" chapter. If you're short on time, try our "6 Quick Challenges" at the start of every chapter. The great thing is that you don't have to worry about what to do. We've given you lots of ideas to try out.

In this book, you'll find hands-on crafts and experiments, thought-provoking prompts for drawing and writing, and plenty of ways to make new discoveries about yourself and the world around you—all from inside your own home! Whenever possible, try using recycled or eco-friendly materials, or reuse items you already have. If you get stuck on a craft or activity, don't worry—you can always move on to another project and come back later, or change the activity to work best for *you*. Remember that this book is about having fun indoors in the ways that you want.

SAFETY FIRST!

Some activities in this book suggest doing online research or asking people questions. Make sure you check with a parent, a teacher, or another grown-up first. Other activities involve working with things that are hot or sharp. Always have an adult present for these projects. We have noted when it is necessary to have a grown-up help you. The most important bit of advice we have for using this book, however, is not to worry about perfection. Be creative! Make mistakes and try again! Most of all, enjoy yourself.

Draw a picture using just your favorite color.

Quick Challenges
ALL ABOUT YOU

Write a poem using only words that start with the letters in your name.

_____

_____

_____

_____

Start a journal in which you just write one line each day.

Draw a self-portrait here
using geometric shapes.

Write down three words you would use to describe yourself. Then list
three words you think friends or family would use to describe you. Are
they the same or different?

_____   _____

_____   _____

_____   _____

Write a letter to your future self, and then put it away
for a year—or five!

Start a Scrapbook

Create a keepsake book full of memories, art, and some of your favorite things.

You can use lots of different books as the base for your scrapbook, such as a store-bought scrapbook, an old book that you repurpose, or a book you make yourself. If you'd like to try creating your own book, follow the steps below.

You Need

- 25 8½-by-11-inch pieces of paper or equally sized craft paper
- Stapler
- Recycled cardboard
- Scissors
- Hole punch
- Ruler
- Pencil
- Ribbon or string
- Materials for decoration, such as recycled fabric, markers, paint, glue, etc.

1. Take five pieces of paper and turn them horizontally so that one of the long edges is on top.

2. Staple these five pieces together twice along the left-hand side, about half an inch from the edge. The staples should be parallel to the edge of the paper.

3. Repeat steps 1 and 2 until you have five separate paper booklets.

4. Have an adult help you cut out two identical pieces of cardboard. Each piece should be the same size as your booklets.

5. Punch three holes along the short left-hand side of each of the booklets and cardboard pieces. Try to keep the holes in the same place each time—you can use the ruler to help you measure where each hole should go so the holes line up when everything is stacked together.

6. Stack your pieces so that the five booklets are in between the two pieces of cardboard and the holes are lined up.

7. Tie a piece of ribbon or string through each hole to bind your book.

8. Decorate your book.

My Scrap Book

Tip!
A scrapbook is the perfect place to use up crafting odds and ends, like leftover yarn and wrapping paper scraps.

WHAT'S IN YOUR SCRAPBOOK?

A scrapbook can be about anything you want—after all, it's *your* book! Do you want it to hold your favorite memories? Photographs only? Or maybe you'd like to include memorabilia like movie ticket stubs, letters you've received, and more. It could even be a tribute to your favorite animal. Use this space to brainstorm.

GETTING SCRAPPY

Check out some of these tried and true ways to scrapbook—or invent some of your own.

Creative Collage

Cut out images from old magazines and newspapers to create new scenes or decorative elements for your scrapbook.

Fantastic Frames

Glue your favorite photographs into your scrapbook, and then decorate them with cute frames made from ribbon, craft sticks, and more.

Elevated Envelopes

Glue several envelopes into your scrapbook so that the openings face up. Decorate the envelopes, and then fill them with mementos like letters or small trinkets.

Scribble Your Feelings

Whatever you're feeling, art can be a great way to express your emotions. Scribble art lets you channel your feelings into a masterpiece!

You Need

- Paper (optional)
- Black marker or pencil
- Colored markers, pencils, or watercolor paint

1. Think of a feeling you are experiencing or a strong emotion you've felt in the past.

2. As you think of this feeling, begin scribbling on the next page or on a separate piece of paper using your marker or pencil. Let your feeling guide you as you create lots of scribbles with loops and lines that cross over each other.

3. Color each section of your scribble drawing. Do this however you want—don't worry about staying in the lines you've drawn.

Once your drawing is finished, take a look at it.
Does it look like the feeling you were thinking about?
Do you feel differently now that you are finished?

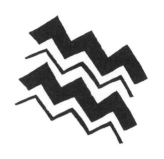

Design a Spectacular City

You're the architect! Draw a fantastic fantasy city in the space below. It could be a futuristic marvel, a woodland city in an enchanted forest, or whatever you decide.

Bring your city to life by building a small version of it. Try including towers and a bridge. What materials will work best for constructing the bridge and towers? How can you keep them from falling? Before you build your city, sketch a draft of it here.

You Need

- Various recycled household materials, such as cups, paper, craft sticks, pencils, etc.

How Do Bridges Hold Weight?

Bridges need to balance two different forces caused by gravity and weight: compression and tension. Compression is a force that pushes or squeezes inward. Tension is a force that stretches or pulls outward. A bridge must be able to balance these forces, spread them out evenly, or transfer them to other areas so the bridge does not break. Most bridges have at least two different parts that do this: abutments and piers. Abutments are the supports that sit at the ends of a bridge. These help direct weight and pressure to the ground on either side of the bridge. Piers are the supports in the middle of a bridge. These channel pressure directly down into the ground.

Make a New Dessert

What do you get when you cross a doughnut with an ice-cream sandwich? A brand-new treat!

DREAM IT

See if you can come up with a brand-new recipe that transforms your favorite desserts into something even better.

First, think about your favorite dessert ingredients and flavors, and list some of them below. How can you combine these in exciting ways to create something different? For example, if you love cherry pie and chocolate brownies, you could create chocolate-cherry brownies. Write down your dessert ideas below, too.

_____

_____

_____

_____

_____

_____

_____

_____

_____

_____

MAKE IT

Now grab an adult and head to the kitchen to experiment. What delicious new dessert can you make? Once you've created your sweet treat, write down your recipe below, including the ingredients and the steps needed to make the dessert.

Tip!
Try looking at different dessert recipes for inspiration.

Groovy Movies

Jerrod has gotten lost trying to meet his friends at the movie theater—and the previews are almost starting! Can you help him make it in time?

Start

Finish

Lights, camera, action! Design
the poster for a movie about your life.

Create a Club

Joining a club can be a great way to meet new people, learn new things, help your community, and just have fun! And there's no better way to find a club dedicated to your favorite things than to start one yourself. Try these steps below to get started.

WHAT IS YOUR CLUB?

Some clubs focus on teaching and learning new skills. Other clubs allow people to meet and discuss a book or movie that they love. And some are dedicated to causes that their members care about, like cleaning up the local community or helping save a species of animal. Describe your club here.

KEEP IT FOCUSED

Now that you know the basics of what your club will be for, think of what activities it will include and write them out here. For example:

• If it's a movie-watching club, think about how your club will decide what movies to watch. Who will bring the snacks? What types of discussions will you have about the movies?

• If your club is devoted to a cause, think about how you can help that cause. What will you need in order to help? What kind of events can you hold to spread your message?

WHAT IS YOUR CLUB'S NAME?

A catchy name can get potential members interested in your club. For example, if you're starting a book club, you might call it "Book Bonanza." Or if you're creating a club for pizza lovers, you might call it "Pizza Pals." Write some possible names for your club here.

_____

_____

_____

_____

_____

_____

LET'S MEET!

Some clubs meet once a week. Others meet less often. Many book clubs, for example, meet once a month to give their members time to read. What's the right number of meetings per month for your club? Think about if your club should meet at school, a library, your home, or somewhere else.

_____

_____

_____

_____

_____

_____

_____

JOIN THE CLUB!

One way to get people to join your club is to design a fun flyer to hand out to friends and family. Draw a draft of your flyer here.

Make sure it includes all the information your members will need to know, like when you meet and where.

Have a Day of Relaxation

Hanging out indoors can be the perfect time to treat yourself to relaxing activities. Try some of the activities listed here or come up with your own.

MUSIC IN YOUR MIND

What song relaxes you the most? Put the song on and close your eyes. What pictures come to your mind as you listen? When the song finishes, draw the images you thought of here.

CREATE A BOOK NOOK

Find the place in your house that is most relaxing to you. With an adult's permission, set up a cozy nest of cushions, pillows, and blankets, and hunker down with your favorite book or comic.

TAKE A DEEP BREATH

Try some breathing exercises like the ones here. Breathing exercises can help lower stress and increase relaxation.

1. **Nostril Breathing:** Use your finger to press your left nostril closed. Inhale through your right nostril. Then use another finger to press your right nostril closed. Open and breath out through your left nostril. Repeat on the other side. Do this a few times.

2. **Breathing to the Beat:** Inhale for a count of four. Then hold your breath for another count of four. Finally, exhale for a count of four. Repeat several times.

3. **Lion Breathing:** Close your eyes and breathe in deeply so that your chest and belly expand. When you are ready to exhale, open your eyes, spread your fingers, tilt your head back, and stick out your tongue. Breathe out in one loud rush, making a *haaa* sound—almost like a lion roaring.

HANG OUT UPSIDE DOWN

Did you know that hanging upside down for a short time can help lower stress? With an adult's permission, try lying on your back on your bed or couch and letting your head hang upside down off the side. Stay like this for 30 seconds to a minute. Afterward, write down how you feel.

Tip!
If you begin to feel light-headed or dizzy at any point, stop the exercise.

What Is Stress?

You know that stress is a feeling of being overwhelmed or anxious—but what is causing you to feel this way, and why? When you are stressed, your brain sends certain chemical messages to the rest of your body. These messages, called stress hormones, make your heart beat faster, focus your attention, and give you bursts of energy. According to scientists, stress is a survival tactic for many animals. In dangerous situations, the extra energy and focus might help an animal escape. For humans, stress is often caused by things like homework or arguments—but don't worry, you can help control it with relaxation techniques like the ones here.

Make a miniature indoor
bowling set with plastic
cups and a small ball.

Quick
Challenges
FUN AND
GAMES

6

Use the space below to have a tic-tac-toe showdown.

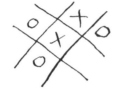

Grab a partner and see how many characters
you can act out using just one accessory,
such as a hat or scarf.

See how many words you can make using only the letters in your name.

_____

_____

_____

_____

A B C D E F G

Hold a game of animal charades: Imitate an animal without making any noise and have a friend or family member guess what it is. Then switch!

Make up a secret handshake and write the steps here.

_____

_____

_____

_____

Put on a Play

Stretch your creativity muscles by creating your very own play. Use the suggestions below to get started—or let your imagination run wild.

PLANNING THE PLAY

Most plays are broken into three parts: the beginning, middle, and end. The beginning sets up who the characters are, what they want, and what the play is about. The middle often introduces some type of problem for the characters to overcome. And the end shows how the characters solve this problem to reach their goal. Try answering these questions and see what you come up with:

1. Where and when does your play take place?

_____

_____

2. Who are your characters?

_____

_____

3. What do your characters want?

_____

_____

4. How do your characters feel about each other?

_____

_____

5. What problem do they encounter?

_____

_____

6. How do they solve it? _____

Next, write a quick description of the main events that happen in each part:

1. Beginning

_____

_____

2. Middle

_____

_____

3. End

_____

_____

Once you've finished, write a short script. Try dividing it into the three parts and tackling one at a time.

AMAZING ACTORS

Take a look around your home, and you're sure to find some awesome actors. Who will you cast?

Ideas:
• Family members
• Friends
• Neighbors
• Stuffed animals
• Yourself!

Tip!
Keep it short! Start with a brief script and a short but fun performance.

Tip!
Ditch the script! If you want, share the answers to your questions and your descriptions with your actors, and let them improvise.

SETTING THE STAGE

Use the space here to design the set for your play.

Take It Further

Have an adult help you set up a temporary stage inside your house. See if you can hang old sheets to act as the curtains at either end of the stage and make fun props out of household and recycled materials.

SUPER SOCKS

Need some extra actors? Why not turn to your laundry basket? Craft some simple sock puppets into any characters you like.

5. After removing your hand from the sock, glue on the buttons, googly eyes, or whatever else you would like to use for eyes.

6. Decorate your sock. You can cut out more fabric for animal ears, use yarn for hair, or do whatever strikes your imagination.

1. Place the sock so it's flat and the sole of the sock is facing up.

2. Have an adult help you cut an oval of fabric about the size of the sock's sole. This will be your character's mouth.

3. Glue the oval to the sole and let dry.

4. Place the sock puppet on your hand so that the mouth is over your palm. Curl your fingers downward to close the mouth. Now decide where you would like to place the eyes, and mark the spots with a marker.

Paper Airplane Race

Tip!
Try adding a paper clip to the nose of your airplane and see if it flies differently.

There isn't always much space to race inside—at least, not for people! Try making these paper airplanes. Then set up a starting and finish line, launch the planes from the starting line, and see which one wins.

Take It Further

Don't feel like racing? Use your airplane to send someone a nice note from across the room!

You Need

- 8½-by-11-inch piece of paper
- Paper clip (optional)

1. Fold the piece of paper in half horizontally so that one short side meets the other.

2. On one side, fold the front corner down so it meets the edge. Repeat on the other side.

3. Fold each long side down to the folded edge to create wings.

4. Pop each folded wing back up part way so that they lie flat.

5. If you want, decorate your plane.

6. Repeat to make as many planes as you'd like.

Step 1

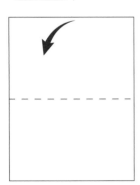

Step 2

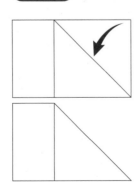

Step 3

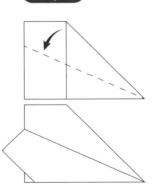

Imagine you are creating the fastest plane in the world. What does it look like? Where is it going? Draw it here.

The Shape of Flight

Have you ever wondered why some birds fly faster than others, or why some planes are super speedy? One of the things that helps an object fly quickly is *aerodynamics*. Aerodynamics refers to the way objects move through the air. When an object flies, it encounters resistance from the air, known as drag. But some shapes and materials help reduce this drag, letting the object fly faster.

Penguin Playtime

This penguin is ready to go for a swim! Help guide her down the iceberg and to the water.

Start

Finish

What do you think a penguin's favorite game would be? Underwater tag? Iceberg hockey? Or a brand-new game? Draw it here.

Drawing Games

Have a blast with these art-based games.

FEEL IT OUT

Sit with your back to a friend or family member. Have that person trace out a simple drawing on your back with their finger. Draw what you think they are drawing here or on a separate piece of paper. Then switch turns.

CAN YOU PICTURE IT?

Have a friend or family member pick an item, such as an object in the room, an animal, or a type of food. The person should then describe this item in detail, without ever saying what it is. Try drawing what they describe here, and then guess what the item is.

Take It Further

If you have more than one friend or family member present, try combining this drawing game with a game of telephone. Have the first person use whispers to describe the object to the second person. The second person should then pass on what they heard to the third person, and so on, until it reaches the artist. See what drawing you end up with!

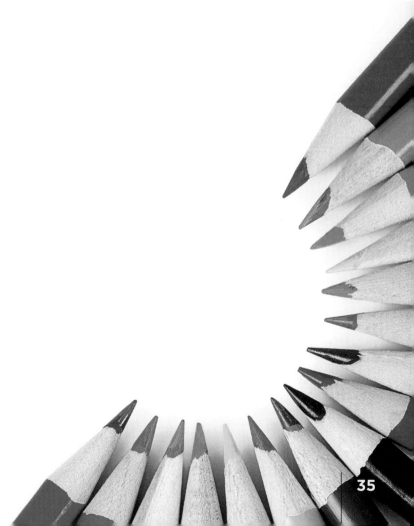

Make Your Own Game

Design a board game you've never seen before. It could be anything from a pirate-themed game to a new version of checkers to a game you design from scratch. Sketch it here.

Take It Further

Bring your board game to life by decorating a recycled piece of cardboard with markers or paper. Use small items you find around the house—such as coins or buttons—for the pieces, or craft pieces out of paper or clay.

Write out some rules to the game here.

_____

_____

_____

_____

_____

_____

_____

_____

Invent a new type of rock-paper-scissors with different objects. Each of those objects must beat one of the other objects with no repeats. For example, fire-sponge-water: fire beats sponge, sponge beats water, and water beats fire. Make up hand signs for each object and draw them here.

Making Magic

Astound your friends and family with a magic show. Set up your performance space. Then come up with a fantastic magician's outfit—don't forget the towel for a cape—and perform some magic tricks. Try the easy tricks below or invent your own.

Rubber Pencil

Trick your audience into believing that you've turned a pencil into rubber! Hold the middle of the pencil loosely between your thumb and pointer finger. The pencil should be loose enough that it will wiggle when you shake it, but not so loose that it falls from your grasp. Quickly shake your hand up and down—the pencil will look like it is made of rubber.

Disappearing Coin

Ahead of time, use a piece of foil to create a fake quarter. First, rub the foil over a real quarter and around its rim. Then cut the impression it leaves into a coin shape. At a quick glance, it will look real! Hold the fake coin in your palm with three real coins and show your audience that you have "four" coins. Close your hand so that the foil crumples into a ball under the three real coins. When you open your hand, it will look like you have only three coins, and that the fourth has "disappeared." (In reality, the foil ball should be hidden under the three real coins. This may take some practice to get right!)

Magic Slices

Make your audience think you used magic to slice a banana through its peel. Ahead of time, gather your banana and a clean pin. Poke the pin through the peel and into the banana. Stop just before you hit the peel on the other side. Now move the pin back and forth from side to side. Pull out the pin. Do this multiple times down the length of the banana. When you show your audience the banana, they won't notice the small pin holes. Say a magical word, such as *abracadabra*, and then peel the banana to show that it has been "magically" sliced. Afterward, eat the banana or freeze the pieces to use later.

A magician has made a rabbit disappear inside a magic hat. Where do you think the rabbit went? Make up a tale about the rabbit's adventure.

Cool Competitions

Can you spot all the items that don't
belong at the bowling alley?

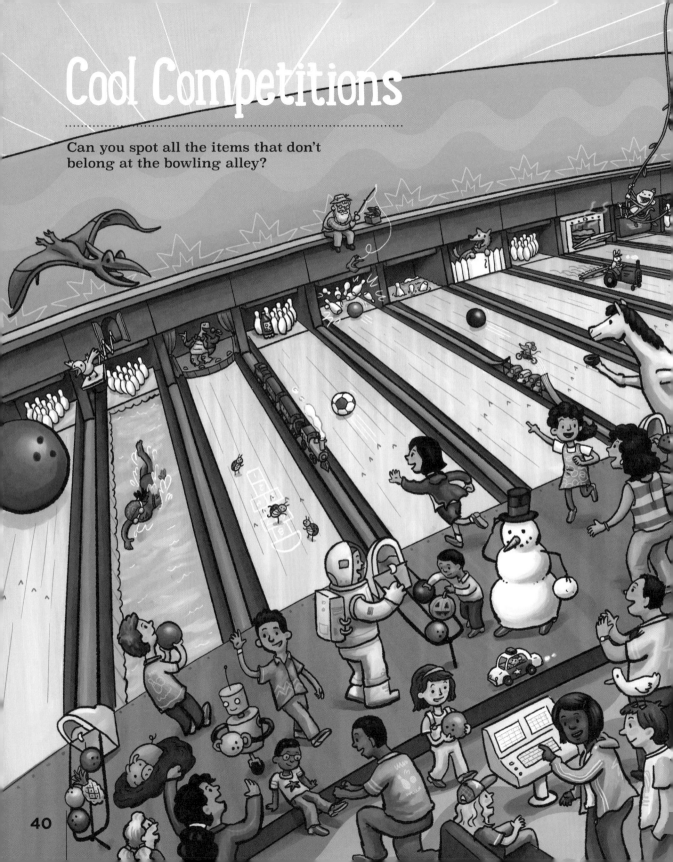

From hot dog eating to pumpkin chucking, the world is full of wacky competitions. Dream up a new one, and then draw it here and write down the rules.

Hot Dog Eating

Participants chow down on as many hot dogs as possible in 10 minutes.

Swamp Soccer

Contestants play soccer . . . in a pit of mud.

Air Guitar Championships

At these events, people compete to see who can rock out the most— with a pretend instrument!

Pumpkin Chucking

Competitors use devices like slingshots or catapults to fling pumpkins as far as possible.

Build a Card House

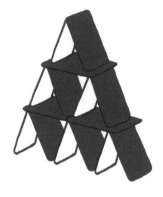

How high can you get your house of cards? Try using these two techniques to get started, and then build the grandest, most amazing house you can think of.

You Need

- At least one deck of playing cards
- Flat surface

TRIANGLE TOWER

1. Lean two cards against each other to form an upside-down V tower.

2. Make another upside-down V tower parallel to the first, about one to two inches away.

3. Add a roof by lying a card flat so it balances on top of the two towers.

4. Keep going—make another tower parallel to the second, about one to two inches away. Add a roof between this tower and the second.

5. Build your next layer—add a tower on top of the flat roof.

6. Try experimenting with a bigger base or more rows of bases to see how tall your house can get.

SPRAWLING HOUSE

1. Start with two cards. Balance the cards against each other in a slightly off-center T shape. The cards should be balancing on their long sides rather than on their short sides. The top of the T is card 1, and the bottom is card 2.

2. Place another card, card 3, slightly off-center of card 2 to form another T shape. The three cards together should form a U shape.

3. Now, place a fourth card slightly off-center to form a T shape with card 3. Altogether, the cards should now form a box shape that doesn't completely close.

4. Keep repeating this shape, building out until the base of your card house is as big as you want.

5. Add a roof by laying cards flat on top of your foundation.

6. Build another layer.

What would your house of cards look like as a real building? Think about its height and shape, how many doors and windows it would have, and whether someone would live there or if it would be used for something else. Draw it here.

List the top five places where you would like to travel.

_____

_____

_____

_____

_____

Quick Challenges
AMAZING ADVENTURES

Imagine one object in your room could teleport you anywhere you wanted to go. Which object would it be? Draw it here.

You just found a buried treasure in your backyard! What jaw-dropping items are part of the treasure? Draw them here.

Draw three items that you would absolutely need to bring on your next adventure.

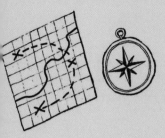

Imagine you are leading a mission to Mars. Write a brief entry here for your captain's log.

_____

_____

_____

_____

Write a short poem using only words that you can make from the letters in the word *adventure*.

_____

_____

_____

_____

_____

_____

_____

Fantastic Forts

Draw the most amazing secret fort that you can imagine. It might be in a tree, underground, or even under the ocean. Think about who lives there, and if anyone—or anything—is guarding it.

Now sketch an indoor version of your fort made from things found right in your home.

With an adult's permission, build your own indoor fort.
Try the ideas below or come up with your own.

BLANKET FORT

Gather up any blankets or sheets you can use. Find a good spot to drape them. For example, drape them between two or more tall pieces of furniture. Make sure to secure their edges so that they don't fall while you're inside! In the space below the draped blankets or sheets, set up a comfy area with more blankets, pillows, and cushions.

TABLE FORT

With an adult's help, drape a large blanket or cloth over a table big enough for you to sit under. Set up a comfy area underneath with blankets, pillows, and cushions.

ART FORT

If you have a large cardboard box on hand, try turning it into an art zone by decorating and drawing on the inside of the box. See how much of the box's walls you can cover with your masterpieces.

What are the rules of your fort? Think some up and list them here.

Explore a Volcano

Imagine that you have been assigned to explore a newly discovered volcano. During your adventure, you come upon something amazing—and totally unexpected. What is it? Write about your journey and what you've found.

You've discovered an amazing volcano—only instead of lava, it erupts something else! Is it diamonds? Gummy candies? Socks? Draw it here.

How Do Volcanos Erupt?

Deep inside a volcano, there is often something called magma. This magma is superhot, semiliquid molten rock. Magma can be found beneath the outermost part of the Earth, called the crust—the part where we all live. When magma builds up in a volcano, the pressure increases. Sometimes, the magma escapes in little bits at a time through vents in the volcano. Other times, the magma has nowhere to escape—and so pressure builds and builds until it explodes in an eruption of lava and ash.

Super Scavenger Hunt

Have an awesome indoor adventure with this scavenger hunt. See how many of these items you can find around your home, and list what they are.

TRY TO FIND . . .

• Three things that start with the letter *U*

_____

• Something bright pink

_____

• Something that has writing in a language you don't speak

_____

• An item older than you are

_____

• Three different types of coins

_____

• An image of a cat

_____

• The softest item in your home

_____

• Something spooky

_____

• Something funny

_____

• A rainbow

_____

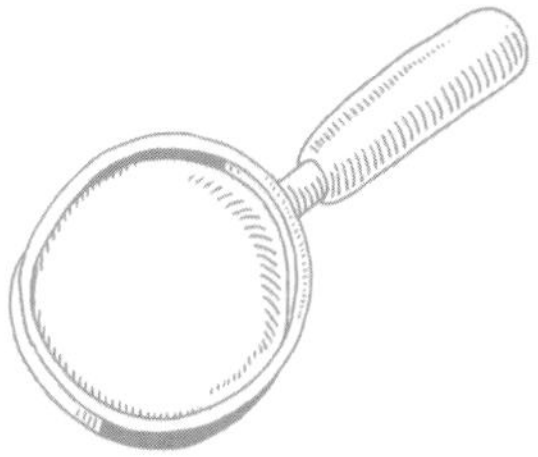

Create a scavenger hunt for a friend or family member.
List the items they must find below.

_____

_____

_____

_____

_____

_____

_____

_____

_____

_____

_____

_____

_____

_____

Snowy Adventure

It's so cold today, even the kittens are bundled up.
Can you find the 20 MITTENS hidden in this picture?

You are exploring a snowy mountain when you come across a mythical creature believed to exist only in legends. What is it?

Have your own indoor snow adventure with this recipe for fake snow!

You Need

- Bowl
- Spoon or spatula
- 3 cups baking soda
- ½ cup white conditioner or white foam shaving cream

Mix the baking soda with either the conditioner or shaving cream until it is blended. Sculpt it into whatever snow shapes you would like.

Top Secret Mission

Prepare for a secret mission by learning how to write in code. Check your answers on page 158.

ALPHABET SWAP

Write out the first 13 letters of the alphabet in a line. Below that, write out the second 13 letters so each letter lines up with the one above it. When you write a message using this code, swap each letter you would normally use with the one directly above or below it in these rows of letters. (So, for example, *A* becomes *N*, and *N* becomes *A*.)

Try Decoding This: PENPX GUR PBQR.

_____

_____

_____

_____

_____

WRITE IN REVERSE

Try writing your words in reverse letter order. You can also reverse the order of the words in each sentence—or reverse the order of the entire message.

Try Decoding This: TUO TI YRT.

_____

_____

BE BOLD

With this code, sentences contain letters written in bold. When read together, the bold letters make other words. For example, the secret word in the following sentence is *code*: The **c**at d**o**ve after the **d**ark gre**e**n mouse. If multiple hidden words are included in the code, you will need to figure out where the spaces between words are.

Try Decoding This: TE**N** TINY, LUCKY **E**AGLES **J**UGGLED TW**O** **B**ALLS.

_____

_____

_____

_____

Write a top secret letter using one of the codes here—or create your own.

CONFIDENTIAL
★ ★ ★
TOP SECRET
★ ★ ★
CONFIDENTIAL

MAKE YOUR OWN INVISIBLE INK

Try this easy recipe to craft the perfect ink for sending secret messages.

You Need

- Lemon or lime
- Knife
- Bowl
- Water
- Spoon
- Cotton swab or paintbrush
- Paper
- Nearby lamp

1. Have an adult help you cut the lemon or lime in half and squeeze its juice into the bowl.

2. Add a few drops of water and stir. This is your ink.

3. Dip your cotton swab or paintbrush into the ink and use it to write your message on a piece of paper. Let it dry.

4. To reveal the hidden message, hold the paper close to the heat of a light bulb or other heat source. The heat will make the ink visible!

Other Inks

Throughout history, people have come up with many ways to write secret messages. In fact, people have been making and using invisible inks for more than 2,000 years! During the American Revolutionary War, leaders and soldiers often used ink made from various chemicals. They would write their secret letters in between the lines of other not-so-secret letters. Then they would mark the letters with either an *F* or an *A*—this let the person receiving the letter know how to reveal the secret message: either by putting it near the heat of a fire or using a special acid mixture.

Use your invisible ink to draw a secret picture here. Do you think it is difficult to draw with the invisible ink? Will the picture look like what you meant to draw when you reveal it?

Dive In

There are so many fish in the sea—how many can you find? See if you can spot the names of the fish below in this word search.

Word List

- ANGEL
- BASKING
- BLUE
- BRAMBLE
- BULL
- COOKIE-CUTTER
- COPPER
- GOBLIN
- GREAT WHITE
- HAMMERHEAD
- HORN
- LEMON
- LEOPARD
- MAKO
- NERVOUS
- NURSE
- POCKET
- SAND TIGER
- SAW
- SLEEPER
- SPINY DOGFISH
- THRESHER
- WEASEL
- WHALE
- ZEBRA

```
G N I K S A B N Z E B R A I
O F I N M A K O H T J L U R
G G R E A T W H I T E N U B
C O O K I E C U T T E R P E
D R A P O E L C T J B E R L
T T W M Q J E L E A R P E A
H E E S V T G E K W A P G H
R E A S U T N M C S M O I W
E T S H N O A O O L B C T N
S H E U U A V N P L L U D U
H S L E E P E R I U E S N R
E C S E H O R N E B U N A S
R H S I F G O D Y N I P S E
T A I L H A M M E R H E A D
```

Splash! Imagine you've shrunk to a miniature size and are on a scuba diving adventure in a tide pool. What do you see? Draw it here.

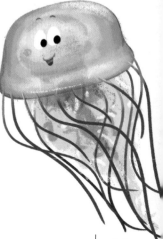

Write a four-line poem about your
favorite animal.

_____

_____

_____

_____

Quick
Challenges
GO WILD

Draw a flower with as many petals as you can.

Draw an animal with a pattern that doesn't exist in nature.

With an adult's permission, watch an animal cam streaming from a
zoo or animal rescue. Record interesting behavior you see.

_____

_____

_____

_____

Write down the smallest animal you can think of, and the
biggest. What would happen if they swapped sizes?

_____

_____

_____

_____

Pick a comfy spot near a window: How many animals can you see outside?
What animals do you think are outside your window right now that you can't see?

_____

_____

_____

Fish School

Help this clown fish reach its anemone—can you find the right way?

Imagine that a school of fish was really a school *for* fish—what would it be like? Write down an underwater class schedule for fish students or a short story from the perspective of a fish in school.

Stretch Like an Animal

Stretching and yoga poses can help lower stress and improve strength, concentration, flexibility, and balance—in fact, animals stretch, too! Try these fun yoga poses inspired by different animals.

FLAMINGO POSE

Stand with your feet hip-width apart and your toes facing forward. Bring the palms of your hands together in front of your heart and breathe in. Focus on a spot in front of you and breathe out. Slowly bring the sole of one foot to rest on your standing leg so that your knee is pointing out to the side. Make sure the sole of your foot stays either above or below the knee. Try to balance while breathing in and out. When you are ready, bring your foot back to the ground. Repeat on the other side.

This pose strengthens your legs and stomach muscles and improves your balance.

DOWNWARD DOG POSE

Start on your hands and knees. Place your palms flat on the floor, shoulder-length apart. Breathe in. Breathe out. Place the bottoms of your toes against the floor and slowly push off the ground, lifting your knees. As you press down through your feet, gently reach your rear end up to the ceiling so that you form an upside-down V. Relax your head and neck and look between your legs. Breathe in and out at your own pace. Come out of the pose after a few seconds.

This pose strengthens your arms and shoulders and stretches your legs.

COBRA POSE

Lie on the carpet, a yoga mat, or a soft blanket on your stomach with your legs and arms straight out behind you. Breath in and out. Place your palms flat on the ground next to your shoulders. Take a big breath in and slowly lift your head, chest, and shoulders off the ground, very gently arching your back and keeping the top of your head reaching up to the ceiling. Breathe out as you lie back down. Repeat as many times as you like.

This pose stretches your chest and back.

Think of an animal besides a flamingo, dog, or cobra. With an adult's supervision, research the animal online or in a book and see how they move. Then, with the help of an adult, come up with a stretch or pose based on the animal and try it out. When you're done, draw it here.

Make a Terrarium

Bring nature inside by making your own terrarium, a miniature garden in a container.

You Need

- Large, clear container such as a glass jar or bowl or a recycled plastic container
- Enough pebbles to fill the bottom of your container
- Activated charcoal (optional)
- Potting soil
- Hand shovel or large spoon
- Small plants that do well indoors (see tips)
- Small items for decorations, such as toys, pretty rocks, or crafting materials
- Spray bottle of filtered water

1. Fill your container with a layer of pebbles about two to three inches high.

2. Activated charcoal can help keep harmful bacteria from growing in the soil. If you are using it, add a thin layer—about half an inch—over the pebbles.

3. Using the shovel or spoon, fill the container about halfway with potting soil.

4. Gently add your plants to the container.

5. Now add your decorations however you like.

6. Use your spray bottle to mist the plants until the soil is moist (or follow directions that may have come with the plants).

7. Place your terrarium near a window in indirect light.

Terrarium Plants

Plants that are small and slow growing tend to work best in terrariums, as do plants that don't need a lot of light. Try these suggestions:
- Moss
- Succulents
- Bird's nest ferns
- Air plants
- Spider plants

Use this space to make notes or keep observations about your terrarium. See if you notice whether some plants seem better suited for it than others and which plants are growing the fastest. What else do you notice?

BUG'S-EYE VIEW

What do you think your terrarium would look like from a bug's perspective?
Draw what the bug might see here.

BUG TALE

Now write a story about a bug's day. Does it live in a garden with lots of tiny neighbors? Is it protecting the garden from other bugs? Does it go on an adventure?

Good Garden Bugs

Many insects don't just live in gardens—they help them! Check out how some of these bugs keep gardens blooming and healthy.

- **Bees:** Bees help flowers bloom because they carry pollen from one flower to another in search of something to eat.
- **Ladybugs:** These spotted beauties often eat bugs that can be harmful to plants, such as aphids.
- **Spiders:** Like ladybugs, spiders find insects tasty, including many that eat or damage plants.

_____

_____

_____

_____

_____

_____

_____

_____

_____

_____

_____

 _____

Dog Daze

Woof! Can you find all the dogs breeds from the word list in this word seach?

Word List
BEAGLE
BOXER
BULLDOG
DACHSHUND
~~DALMATIAN~~
GREAT DANE
GREYHOUND
HUSKY
POODLE
PUG
SETTER
SHEEPDOG
SHEPHERD
SPANIEL
TERRIER

```
Q S S H E E P D O G
W H B U L L D O G R
B E A G L E Z Z R E
S P A N I E L Q E Y
E H U S K Y Q F A H
T E R R I E R W T O
T R B O X E R Q D U
E D A L M A T I A N
R D A C H S H U N D
P U G P O O D L E Z
```

Bowwow—that's a lot of dog breeds! With an adult's help, do some research to learn about different dog or cat breeds. Then dream up an entirely new breed of dog or cat.

What does this new breed of dog or cat look like? Draw it below:

What is the breed called?

_____

_____

_____

_____

What special characteristics does this breed have?

_____

_____

_____

_____

Animal Habitats

Imagine you are exploring a superhot desert, the icy North Pole, or a deep, dark ocean trench. Suddenly you spot a brand-new animal species. Give your animal a name and describe how its features help it live in its habitat. Perhaps it has thick fur to help it stay warm or big eyes to see well in the dark . . . or maybe it has some never-before-seen features!

_____

_____

_____

_____

_____

Amazing Adaptations

Many animals have body parts or other features that make them well-adapted to extreme habitats. Check out a few of them here:

- **Red panda**: When it gets cold, red pandas can wrap themselves in their thick, fluffy tails for warmth.
- **Fennec fox:** A fennec fox's extra-furry paws act almost like snowshoes to keep it from sinking into shifting sand.
- **Colossal squid:** This deep-sea animal has giant eyes that let it see in inky-black waters.

Draw the animal you discovered here and label its special features.

A Tall Tail

Add some unusual, adorable, or completely unexpected tails to these animals!

Create animals with wild tails by making your own marshmallow animal models.

You Need

- Small marshmallows
- Large marshmallows
- Paper straws
- Scissors
- Items to decorate your creature, such as colorful paper, markers, feathers, sprinkles, or anything else you want to use

Using your materials, try to build animal models out of the marshmallows and straws. Your models should each have a head, four limbs, a body, and a tail. (You can use scissors to cut the straws into smaller pieces if you'd like.) Then start decorating! Add spots, stripes, spikes, feathers, and more to make a terrific tail.

A Tail's Tale

Why do animals have tails? Scientists think that one of the most basic reasons is for balance. Unlike humans, many animals walk or crawl on four legs. Their tails help them stay balanced in this position. Tails can also help certain animals steer through water. And on top of that, many animals use their tails to communicate. For example, a dog might wag its tail up high when it wants to play.

Plan a Pet Party

Plan the ultimate bash for your pet—or a pet you wish you had! What would the decorations and invitations to the party look like? Draw them here.

Create a gift list and a guest list for your pet's
(or dream pet's) birthday party.

_____

_____

_____

_____

_____

_____

_____

_____

Describe the cake you will serve at this celebration.
What will it be made of? What will it look like?

_____

_____

_____

_____

_____

_____

PET GIFTS

Create a rope toy for your favorite dog or make a dog-themed picture frame to show off your furry BFF. (If you don't have pets, you may also consider donating the rope toy to an animal shelter or giving the rope toy and frame to a friend or family member with pets.)

DOGHOUSE PICTURE FRAME

You Need

- Small snack box or tissue box
- Scissors
- Construction paper
- Glue
- Photo to frame
- Markers
- Toilet paper tube
- White construction paper or cardstock

1. Cut off the top of the snack or tissue box.

2. Cut a triangle shape out of the construction paper for the roof of the doghouse. Glue this to the top of the box.

3. Glue your photo onto the box and decorate the box.

4. To add a bone to the front, cover the tube in white construction paper or cardstock. Cut out two pieces shaped like the ends of a bone and glue those to the ends of the tube. Once it is all dry, glue the bone to the front of the box.

DOGGY ROPE TOY

1. Have an adult help you cut nine equal strips of felt or fabric. For an average-size dog, make the strips about four feet long and two inches wide. You can make these smaller or larger for different-sized dogs.

2. Line up all your strips next to each other and tie them together in a secure knot at one end.

3. Separate the strips into three groups of three strips.

4. Braid the first group of three strips and secure it with a knot at the bottom.

5. Repeat with the second and third groups.

6. Now braid the small three braids into one larger braid. Secure at the bottom with a knot.

See how many U.S. states you can list here without looking any up.

_____

_____

_____

_____

_____

_____

Quick Challenges BOOST YOUR BRAIN

How many triangles can you see in this image?

(answer: 27)

Try to think of a vegetable or fruit that begins with each letter of the alphabet.

_____

_____

_____

_____

Taco cat spells the same thing forward and backward. Can you create another word or phrase that is the same forward and backward?

_____

_____

_____

_____

Solve this riddle: I appear once in a minute, twice in a moment, and never in one thousand years. What am I?

(answer: the letter M)

Can you draw this shape without lifting your pencil from the paper?

Picture This

Can you solve these visual word puzzles? Take a look at the example in number one, then see if you can figure out answers to the rest.

1

C
A
L
M

ANSWER:
CALM DOWN

2

LEFT
PIZZA

ANSWER:

3

THEwalkingRAIN

ANSWER:

4

THINK U SPEAK

ANSWER:

5

DANCE
DANCE   DANCE
DANCE

ANSWER:

6

WRONG
+WRONG
———————
RIGHT

ANSWER:

7

DAST 4

ANSWER:

8

VISION VISION

ANSWER:

9

CLOUD
TH

ANSWER:

Now look at the phrases below. Come up with your own clever visuals to express them, using the Picture This puzzle for inspiration. Then think of a common phrase on your own to draw.

JUST IN TIME   **UNDERCOVER SPY**   **ROUND OF APPLAUSE**

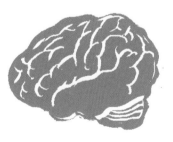

Tongue Twisters

See if you can say each of these tongue twisters three times, fast!

Pink poodles plodded through oodles of puddles.

A sleek snake sneaks six stacked slacks.

Kerry the bear bears little care for buried berries.

Come up with some of your own tongue twisters and write them here.

_____

_____

_____

_____

_____

_____

Tip!
Try playing with words that start with the same letter or rhyme.

Pick your favorite silly tongue twister (or make your own) and draw the scene it is describing here.

A-maze-ing Mazes

Help this hungry hamster reach its treat!

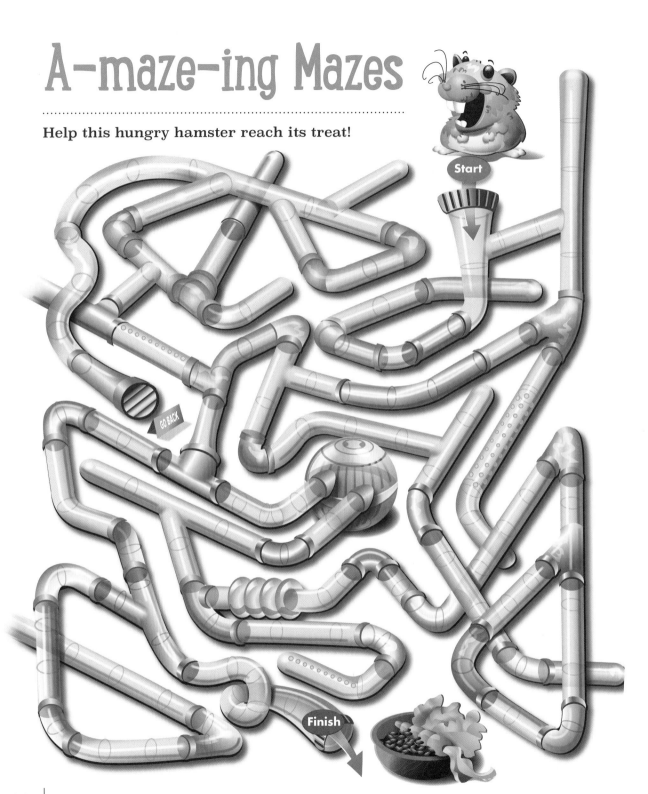

BUILD A 3-D MAZE

Make a 3-D maze that changes every time you do it. Play it yourself or challenge your friends and family.

You Need

- Scissors
- Poster board
- Shoebox lid
- Pencil or pen
- Ruler
- Wide straws
- Hole punch
- Metal fasteners
- Sticky notes
- Marble

1. Cut out a piece of poster board the same size as the shoebox lid. You can trace the lid on the poster board to see how large it is.

2. Decorate the poster board if you would like.

3. Draw a grid on the back of the piece of poster board, with each line about two inches from the next. Poke a hole in each spot where the lines intersect.

4. Cut wide straws into three-inch pieces. Punch a hole in each piece, about one inch from one of its ends.

5. Use metal fasteners to attach the straws to the front of the poster board, as shown below.

6. Write START and FINISH on two separate sticky notes. Place them at different spots on the poster board.

7. Fit the poster board inside the shoebox lid.

8. Create a new maze each time you play by rotating the straws. Place a marble on START. The goal is to get the marble to the finish line.

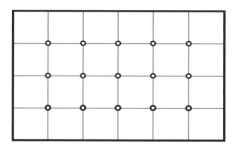

DESIGN A MAZE

Now create your own standard maze. Draw it on the next page either freehand or using the tips below.

You Need

- Ruler or other straight edge
- Pencil
- Eraser

1. Using the ruler or straight edge, draw a large rectangle.

2. Erase a very small section of the border on two sides of the rectangle. These spaces are normally placed on opposite ends of the rectangle but can be anywhere you want. The spaces are your start and finish.

3. Just inside your large rectangle, create a smaller rectangle. Use your pencil to erase several small spots along the border. These are holes in the "walls" of your maze.

4. Add one to two more smaller rectangles inside the first ones. Use your eraser to add holes in the walls.

5. Continue adding walls and making holes until the maze is filled in.

6. Using your pencil, very lightly mark out the path that you want to lead from start to finish.

7. Add dead ends throughout your maze that block all other routes.

8. Erase the path you have made.

9. Give the maze to a friend or family member to solve.

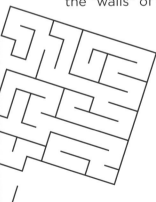

Trivia Time

Boost your brain with this trivia quiz. Don't worry if you don't get all—or any!—of the answers right; the fun part is learning something new.

1. Which marine mammal can dive the deepest?
a. Sea lion
b. Cuvier's beaked whale
c. Blue whale
d. Sea otter

2. How many stars and stripes are on the American flag?
a. 25 stars and 25 stripes
b. 48 stars and 13 stripes
c. 50 stars and 13 stripes
d. 50 stars and 50 stripes

3. In which present-day country were the first-ever ancient Olympics held?
a. Guatemala
b. Italy
c. Greece
d. None of the above

4. About how many miles can the sound of a lion's roar travel?
a. 1
b. 3
c. 5
d. 10

5. True or False: On some planets, it can rain diamonds.

6. In which country were the oldest known human-created mummies found?
a. Chile
b. Egypt
c. Sudan
d. Iceland

7. How many muscles are in a cat's ear?
a. 3
b. 10
c. 32
d. 300

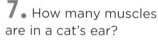

8. True or False: Lightning can be hotter than the surface of the sun.

9. How many hearts does an octopus have?
a. 0
b. 1
c. 3
d. 25

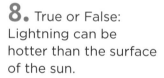

10. True or False: Astronauts can see the Great Wall of China from space.

Create your own quiz! First, think about what type of quiz you want to make. It could focus on any subject, from dogs to sports to world leaders. It could also be a general trivia quiz that covers all sorts of topics. Do some research to find fun facts about your quiz subject. Write a quiz question based on each fun fact and provide multiple answers, including the correct one. Then challenge a friend or family member to give it a go!

Tip!
Write the answer key on a separate piece of paper, and then share the answers with the person you quizzed after they're done!

Research Tips

Try these helpful tips when researching questions and answers for your quiz:

• **Check your sources:** Not every source is reliable! When researching, ask yourself whether you are getting information from a good source. Good sources often include educational or scientific organizations.

• **Use more than one source:** Check multiple sources to verify the information you find.

• **Take notes:** Make sure to mark down where you found your facts.

Animal Shapes

Use the steps below to practice drawing a bunny from geometric shapes. Then use your creativity to turn the shapes on the next page into a whole host of animals.

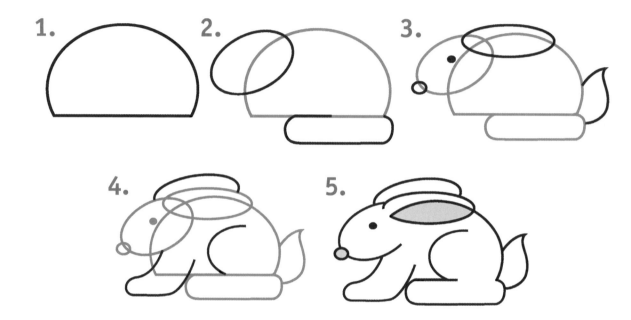

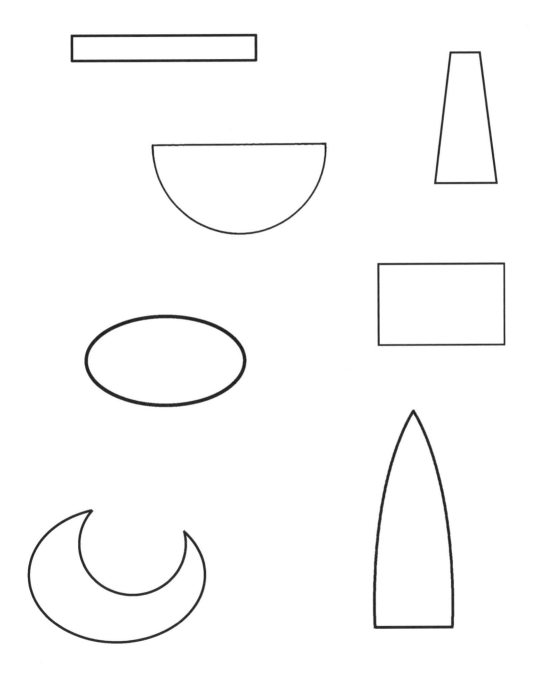

Make a T Puzzle

Stump your friends and family with this simple puzzle that is tougher than it seems.

You Need

- Paper
- Cardboard (optional)
- Scissors
- Pen or pencil

1. Trace or copy the T-shape on the right—including the lines inside of it—onto a separate piece of paper. Cut out the T-shape.

2. If you want, glue the paper onto cardboard to make it sturdier, and trim the cardboard down to match the T-shape.

3. Cut the T into four different shapes by cutting along the lines within the letter.

4. Now trace the line-free T on the next page onto a separate piece of paper. Cut that out as well. (If you want, you can also add this one to cardboard.)

5. Scramble the four cut-up T pieces, and challenge a volunteer to arrange the pieces back into the T-shape. They can look at the line-free T you cut out to see how the completed puzzle is supposed to look.

Tip!
Don't show your volunteer the drawing on this page of the T-shape with lines inside—that will give away the answer!

See if you can create another version of the puzzle with a different letter or shape. Or have a friend create one for you to solve. Do rounded shapes or angled ones work best?

Tummy Troubles

Follow the correct maze path from START to FINISH. Write down the letters you cross along the way and unscramble them to find out what sugary treat caused the fox's tummy ache. (Hint: They're often shaped like rings!)

LETTERS: _ _ _ _ _ _ _ _ _

ANSWER: _____

Write a story about the fox's adventures
and what led up to his tummy troubles.

Name That Number

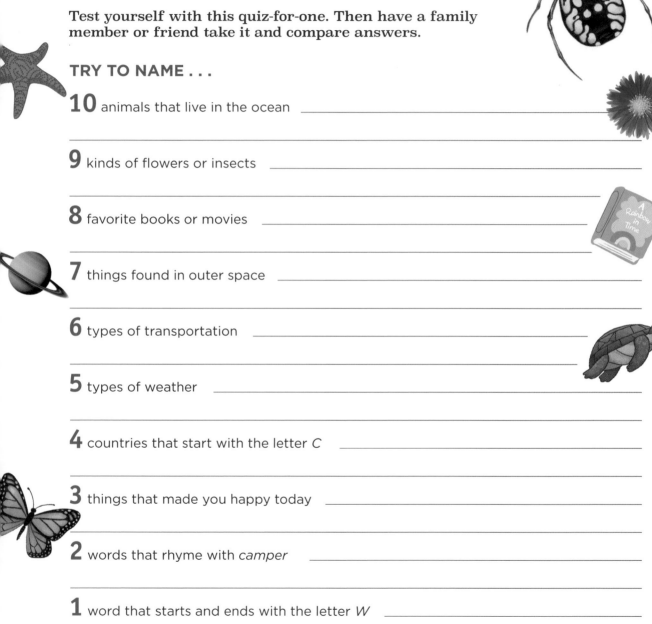

Test yourself with this quiz-for-one. Then have a family member or friend take it and compare answers.

TRY TO NAME . . .

10 animals that live in the ocean _____

_____

9 kinds of flowers or insects _____

8 favorite books or movies _____

_____

7 things found in outer space _____

_____

6 types of transportation _____

5 types of weather _____

_____

4 countries that start with the letter *C* _____

_____

3 things that made you happy today _____

_____

2 words that rhyme with *camper* _____

_____

1 word that starts and ends with the letter *W* _____

_____

Come up with your own number quiz here.

Quick Challenges HELPING OTHERS

Surprise a family member by doing one of their chores for them. Write their reaction here.

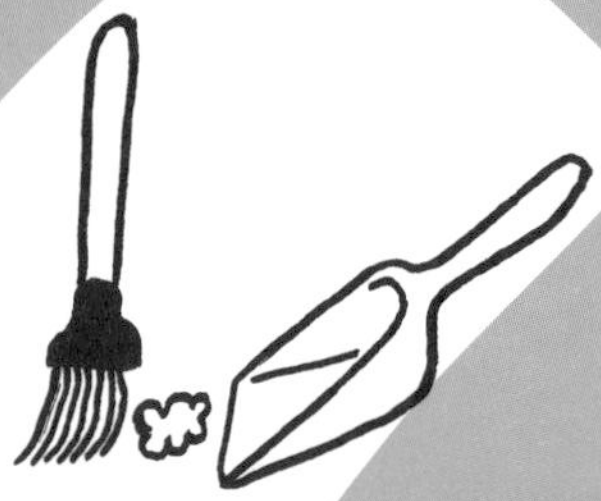

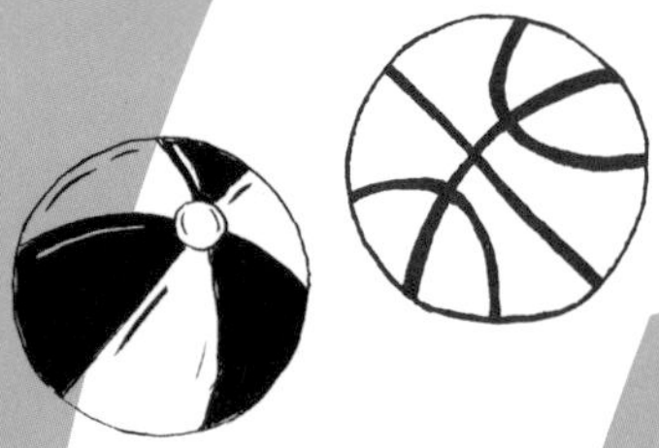

See if there are any old toys, games, or clothes of yours that you would like to donate. List them here.

Write a letter to someone you care about and send it to them.

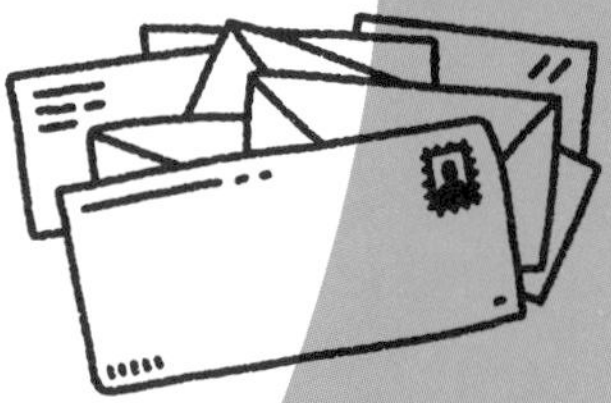

Think about three people who are close to you, and write down something you like about each of them here.

_____

_____

_____

_____

List three ways you and your family could cut back on water or electricity this week.

_____

_____

_____

_____

Gently give yourself a high five in a mirror—it will boost your own mood, letting you be kind to yourself, too!

Write a Letter for an Important Cause

Words can make a difference! Learn how to craft a letter to support a cause you care about.

PICK A CAUSE

First, decide on a cause. Do you care a lot about homeless animals in shelters? Are you passionate about cleaning up pollution in the ocean? There is no wrong answer—there are many ways you can help the world. Write a few lines about this cause here.

_____

_____

_____

_____

DO YOUR RESEARCH

Have an adult help you do some research on your subject. What are some of the ongoing problems for your cause? What are some solutions or ways to help?

_____

_____

_____

Tips!

Look for News Articles: See if there are recent news articles on your subject of interest.
Check the Science: Scientific organizations can provide data and more resources on your topic of interest.
Find Other Helpers: Organizations that are also devoted to your cause are great sources to learn more about how you can help—and how the government can help, too.

WRITE YOUR REPRESENTATIVE

With an adult's help, look up your U.S. senators or local representatives and decide where to send your letter. Who is the best representative to write to? What do you think might make them care about your issue?

> **Tip!**
> With an adult's help you can learn more about elected officials here: **usa.gov/agencies**.

Put the date at the top of the letter.

Type the letter and proofread it.

March 25, 2023

When writing an address, always use the phrase *The Honorable* before a senator or representative's name.

The Honorable Jane Doe
United States Senate
Washington, D.C. 20510

The name and address of the recipient can be found at the website listed above.

Dear Senator Doe,

Explain who you are.

When referring to your representative, use *Senator* or *Representative*.

My name is Edward Gonzalez, and I am a student at Jackson Middle School in Evansville. My class recently learned about the importance of bees. Bees are pollinators, meaning they help many plants grow. In fact, much of the food we eat depends on bees in order to grow! But bees are in danger because of dangerous chemicals found in pesticides. I am writing to ask for your support to make laws that reduce the use of pesticides and protect bees. This is important for both the people of the world and our ecosystems. Thank you.

Sincerely,

End with *Sincerely*.

Edward Gonzalez

Include a thank-you.

Explain the issue you are writing about. Be specific about the problem, and why it is important. Make sure to include possible solutions.

Edward Gonzalez
123 Main Street
Evansville, IN 47702

Include your name and mailing address to get a reply.

Create a Kindness Calendar

Turn helping others into a monthlong (or a yearlong!) activity by creating a calendar of kind acts. Read about some acts of kindness you can do for each of the following categories, and then come up with some of your own.

When coming up with your acts of kindness, think of the following questions:
1. Are there problems I see that I can help solve?
2. What makes me feel good? What would make other people feel happy, too?
3. What would make someone else's day a little bit easier?
4. Is there something I can do or say to encourage or inspire others?

AT HOME

• Ask to help out with cooking dinner or cleaning up.
• Add an extra chore to your normal routine.
• Write kind notes to your family members.

Come up with your own.

_____
_____
_____
_____
_____

IN YOUR COMMUNITY

• Host a bake sale and donate the money to a local charity.
• Go on a walk with a trusted adult, and bring along a trash bag and some rubber gloves. Pick up any trash you see.

Come up with your own.

_____
_____
_____
_____

WITH FRIENDS

• Offer to lend a friend a book, comic, or toy they might like.
• With an adult's permission, host a clothing or toy swap with your friends, and donate anything that's left over.
• Surprise a friend with a meaningful compliment.

Come up with your own.

_____
_____
_____
_____

AT SCHOOL

• Offer to study with a classmate.
• Start a kind acts club.
• Write a teacher a thank-you note.

Come up with your own.

_____
_____
_____
_____

When you have a list of kind acts, plan them out in calendar form.

You Need

- Poster board or cardboard
- Ruler
- Marker
- Decorating materials

Tip!
Start by drawing out a draft of your calendar on the next page. Make sure to include enough space in each block to write your act of kindness.

1. Using a ruler and your marker, draw a grid on your poster board. It should have seven columns and at least six rows, like below.

2. At the top of each column, write the days of the week.

3. Find out on which day of the week the first day of next month falls. Place the number 1 in the first row under the correct day. (So, if the first day of next month falls on a Monday, place the number 1 in the first row under Monday.) Number the rest of the days from there.

4. Start planning: Add acts of kindness to complete throughout the month.

5. Decorate your calendar however you like.

Sunday	Monday	Tuesday	Wednesday	Thursday	Friday	Saturday
	1	2	3	4	5	6
7	8	9	10	11	12	13
14	15	16	17	18	19	20
21	22	23	24	25	26	27
28	29	30	31			

DRAFT YOUR CALENDAR

Draw a draft of your calendar here. Feel free to play
around and add and remove things as you like.

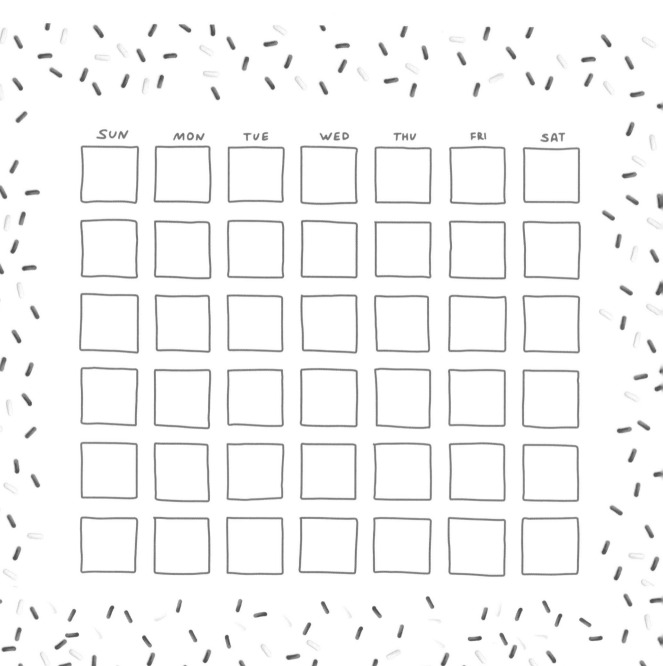

SUN	MON	TUE	WED	THU	FRI	SAT

CREATE A KINDNESS HOLIDAY

Think about what it would be like if one of your days of kindness became a national holiday. In the space below, write down what traditions the holiday would include, what foods people might eat, and more.

_____

_____

_____

_____

_____

_____

_____

_____

_____

_____

_____

_____

_____

_____

Help Clean Up

Cleaning up after yourself is always helpful, and you can make it fun, too, with these cleaning games.

LAUNDRY RACE

Once the laundry is dry, compete with a family member to see who can finish folding clothes the fastest.

CLUTTER DASH

Give yourself three minutes and see who can pick up the most clutter from around the house and put its back in its rightful spot.

"EXCAVATE" YOUR HOME

Pretend you are an archaeologist on an exciting dig. Narrate what you are doing as you sweep up dirt or pick up dirty clothes—describe what you've found as if it is an ancient artifact worthy of being displayed in a museum.

CLEANING HUNT

If you have siblings, create an Easter egg-style hunt for them. Hide small prizes in places around the house—especially under stray toys and clothes—for them to find as they clean.

What is your least favorite chore? Come up with a game that makes it fun. Write down the rules here, and then try it out.

_____

_____

_____

_____

_____

_____

_____

_____

_____

_____

_____

_____

_____

Organization Tips

Keeping things neat or cleaning messy areas can seem overwhelming. Try these tips to make it easier:
- Listen to music while cleaning.
- Create a checklist.
- Break big jobs into smaller parts and do them one at a time.
- Create fun labels or signs for different containers.

Party On!

Can you fit each of these birthday-themed words into the grid?

3 LETTERS
AGE
BOW
HAT

4 LETTERS
GIFT
CAKE
YEAR
CARD

5 LETTERS
PARTY
ICING

6 LETTERS
RIBBON
BANNER
CANDLE

7 LETTERS
BALLOON
PRESENT

8 LETTERS
ICE CREAM
SURPRISE

9 LETTERS
STREAMERS

11 LETTERS
CELEBRATION

Plan an awesome, personalized party for someone you care about. Use the questions listed below to come up with ideas that your special person will love. If you don't know the answers to some of them, see if you can find out.

Who is this party for? _____

_____

What is the occasion—a birthday, congratulations, or something else? _____

_____

Think about things this person loves—what would make a great party theme? For example, would a friend who is a fan of sharks love a shark-themed bash?

_____

_____

What are this person's favorite foods? _____

_____

Would this person prefer to have a small party or a big one? _____

_____

Does this person like surprises? _____

_____

Would this person like to do an activity during the party, like making art or going roller skating? Or would they prefer to hang out and talk with friends? _____

_____

Picture Perfect

Give the gift of a meaningful photograph or drawing in a picture frame decorated by you.

Safety Tip!
Ask an adult for help with anything hot.

UPCYCLED FRAME
Upgrade a regular photo frame by adding your own touches.

You Need

- Low-heat glue gun
- Decorating materials, such as toy figurines, buttons, ribbons, fake flowers, etc.
- Photo frame that's the right size for your picture
- Spray paint (optional)
- Newspaper, to protect your work area (optional)
- Photograph or drawing

1. Pick out the items you want to glue to your frame. These can be small toy figurines or action figures, buttons, ribbons, fake flowers, or whatever you can think of. Use the space below to draft how you would like to arrange these items on your frame.

2. Have an adult help you use the glue gun to glue the items into place.

3. If you want, you can spray-paint the frame to be all one color. (If you do so, make sure to first remove the glass from the frame and lay out newspaper.) You can also add paint, more decorations, environmentally friendly glitter, and more.

4. Let your frame dry completely. Add your picture, and then give it as a gift.

Tip!
Make sure you have permission to use the frame before decorating it.

Some of the best memories happen when there isn't a camera around. Use this space to draw a favorite memory that you *don't* have a photograph of.

Get the Scoop

Create a treasured keepsake by interviewing a loved one and recording their answers. Try asking the questions below, or come up with your own.

How did we meet?

_____

_____

_____

_____

Describe your memory of this meeting.

_____

_____

_____

What is your favorite memory of us together?

_____

_____

_____

What is something that we haven't done together that you would like to try?

_____

_____

_____

_____

What is the best meal we've eaten together?

_____

_____

_____

_____

What is the funniest experience we've had?

_____

_____

_____

Take It Further

Interview several friends and family members and collect their answers in a keepsake memory book.

Help Plan Dinner

Work with an adult to plan out and make a delicious dinner for your family or friends. After answering the questions below, write out your menu on the next page.

PLAN THE MEAL

Will this be a simple meal, or do you want to try something a little more complicated? Are there allergies or dietary needs to consider? Answer the questions below with the help of an adult and decide what you will make.

Who will be at dinner, and how much food will you need?

_____

_____

Does anyone have any special dietary needs or food allergies?

_____

_____

How much time do you have to shop for ingredients and cook?

_____

_____

Menu

Beverages:

Appetizer:

Main Dish:

Side Dish:

Dessert:

SHOPPING LIST

Once you have decided on a menu, look up some recipes and write the ingredients you will need here. What ingredients do you already have and what will you need to get?

_____

_____

_____

_____

_____

_____

_____

_____

_____

_____

_____

_____

_____

_____

_____

_____

SETTING THE SCENE

Make a fancy name card or place setting for each of your guests. Design them here.

Draw an alien inspired by a household object.

Quick Challenges
SUPERCOOL
SCIENCE

Write down which planet you'd most like to visit and why.

_____

_____

_____

_____

Imagine that you are a scientist with a secret lab in your house. Describe your lab here.

_____

_____

_____

_____

If you were a time traveler journeying to the past, what three modern things would you bring with you? List them here.

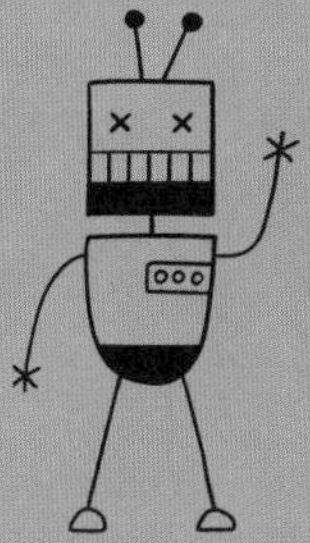

_____

_____

_____

_____

Draw a robot using only geometric shapes.
Give it a name.

See if you can find the oldest piece of technology in your home, and the newest.

_____

_____

_____

_____

Make a Slime Monster

Create a spooky—or cute!—slime monster of your own.

You Need

- Bowl
- Utensil for mixing
- ½ cup liquid glue
- ½ cup water
- Food coloring (any color)
- Eco-friendly glitter (optional)
- ½ teaspoon baking soda
- 1 tablespoon saline solution (contact solution)
- Googly eyes or other decorations, like plastic vampire teeth (optional)

1. Add the glue and water in a bowl and mix together with your utensil.

2. Add several drops of food coloring and the glitter and mix.

3. Add the baking soda and saline solution and mix.

4. Add in the googly eyes or other decorations you chose.

5. Use your hands to knead the slime together. Then enjoy your gooey monster!

Draw the slimiest creature you can imagine.

Hagfish Slime

Also known as slime eels, hagfish are eel-shaped fish that live in cold ocean waters. When a hagfish feels threatened, it secretes large amounts of a slime sticky enough to glue a shark's jaws together! Scientists are studying the slime to see what uses it might have—some even think it can be made into clothing.

Rad Robots

Can you find your way from one end of this robot to the other?

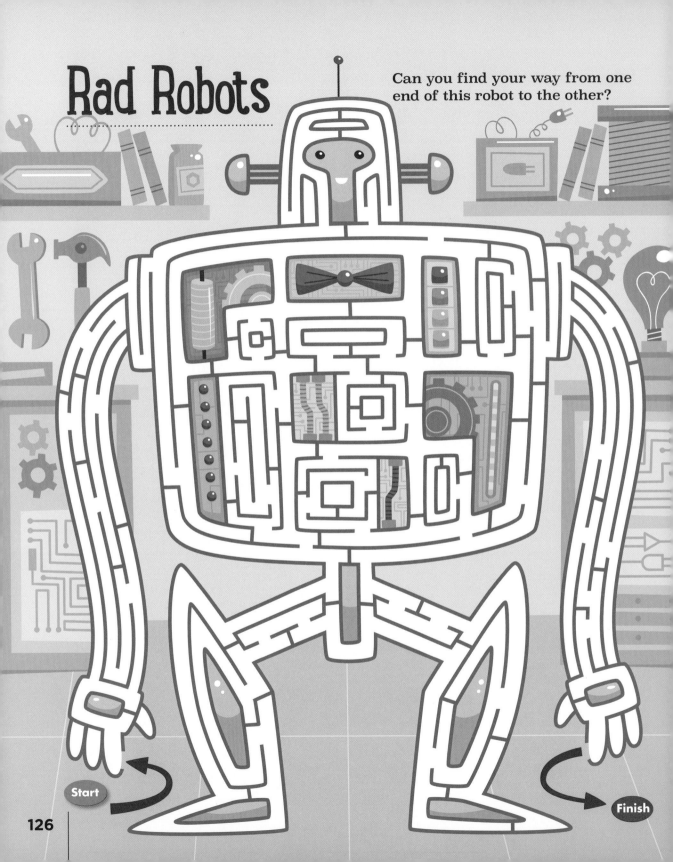

Start

Finish

Design a pet for this robot. Consider whether the pet is another robot or a living critter. Also decide if it's from Earth or an alien planet. What tricks does it know?

Explore an Uncharted Planet

Your home is probably pretty familiar to you. But what would it look like to an alien visiting Earth? Pretend you are a voyager from a far-off planet visiting your home for the first time. Write down some of the things you see but describe them as an alien might. For example, would an alien think a vacuum cleaner is a long-lost robot friend? Would it try to eat the houseplants? Come up with some funny hijinks here.

_____

_____

_____

_____

_____

_____

_____

_____

_____

_____

_____

Draw the front and back of a postcard for alien tourists on Earth to mail home—don't forget the stamp!

Dear _____,

To:

_____

_____

_____

_____

Design a Rocket Ship

Design an amazing rocket ship here.

Describe the cool features your rocket ship has. Maybe it has an indoor pool, or maybe it can translate every language ever spoken—it's up to you.

_____

_____

_____

_____

_____

_____

_____

_____

_____

Life in Space

Astronauts in space need to live in conditions very different from those on Earth. Check out some of the differences here:

- **Meals:** The food that astronauts eat must last a long time, so it is often stored in vacuum-sealed pouches. Astronauts also can't have foods that leave crumbs, as crumbs can drift about in zero gravity and get stuck in equipment, causing problems.

- **Sleep:** Astronauts must strap themselves into sleeping bags in small compartments so they don't drift while snoozing.

- **Showers:** For many astronauts, showering with running water isn't an option in space. Instead, they squirt packets of liquid soap and water onto their skin and use a rinseless shampoo.

Hold a Science Fair at Home

With permission from an adult, set up a science fair in your own home! Invite friends and family to each bring a cool experiment to show off, or prepare stations with different activities that you can all try together.

GATHER YOUR MATERIALS

Make a list of what you might need to hold the fair. Make sure you have access to the things listed below, and add the items that you will need for any experiments.

You Need

- Adult supervision
- Newspaper to place over surfaces
- Towels for cleanup

CREATE INVITATIONS

Draft an invitation or flyer to give to your friends and family. Describe when and where the science fair will be held and what people will need to bring. Should they bring an experiment to share? If so, ask them to be prepared to explain the science behind their project. Or should they come ready to try experiments that you set up?

Set Up Your Space

Set up several tables or areas where you will conduct your experiments. These can all be in the same room or in different rooms. If you are making all the experiments yourself, decorate some signs for each one. If your guests are bringing experiments, put out blank signs for them to fill in.

Try these fun, at-home science experiments to get started—or have an adult help you do some research to come up with your own.

COLORFUL FLOWERS

Learn how plants take in water by making white flowers turn different colors.
Science to research: Capillary action

Safety Tip!
Ask an adult for help with anything sharp.

You Need

- Water
- 3 glasses
- Food coloring in 3 colors
- 3 white flowers (carnations work best)
- Scissors

1. Fill your three glasses halfway with warm water. In each glass, add about 25 drops of a different color of food coloring.

2. Have an adult help you cut the stem of each flower on the diagonal.

3. Place the stem of each flower in a different cup. What happens? Why do you think this is?

Capturing Capillary Action

To get water, plants need to bring moisture in through their roots and stems. They do this using a process called *capillary action*: this is when water is able to move up through a plant without the help of gravity, thanks to forces that attract the liquid water to the solid root and stem. Normally, you can't see water moving up a plant and into its leaves or petals, where it evaporates. But in this experiment, you can see the dye left behind by the water after it evaporates.

CLEANING OLD COINS

Find out which liquids are the best for cleaning old coins—and why.

Science to research: Acidity

You Need

- 3 different liquids, including water, lemon juice, and milk (use more liquids if you'd like, and get creative)
- 3 glasses (or more, depending on how many liquids you choose)
- 3 oily, dirty pennies (or more, depending on how many liquids you choose)
- Clean towel

1. Pour about an inch of each liquid into separate glasses, making sure to label the glasses.

2. Drop a dirty penny into each glass.

3. Wait at least 30 minutes.

4. Remove and wipe off the pennies. Which one is the cleanest? Why do you think that is?

Acid Is the Answer

Pennies are made of a metal called *copper*. Over time, copper starts to lose its shine thanks to something called *copper oxide*. When the molecules in the copper interact with molecules in the air, they create copper oxide: a dull black powder. Because copper oxide dissolves in acid—which can be found in things like lemon juice and vinegar—liquids with more acid in them will clean the pennies the best.

Amazing Inventions

Think of an invention you find amazing, or one you use all the time. It can be anything from a simple paper clip to a video game console. If you could make improvements to this invention, what would they be? Draw your improved invention here.

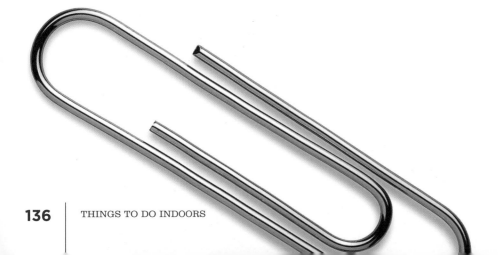

Not everything is what it seems in this laboratory! See if you can find the items listed below in this image.

tack

crescent moon

artist's brush

star

banana

shoe

sock

ruler

pizza

baseball

hammer

fish

teacup

bell

toothbrush

Make Galactic Art

Create your own images of the farthest reaches of our galaxy with these neat art tricks.

ICE ART

You Need

- Ice cube tray
- Water
- Nontoxic liquid watercolor paints
- Utensil for mixing
- Newspaper, to protect your work area
- Watercolor paper
- Soap

1. Fill the ice cube tray with water. Mix a few drops of one paint color into each slot. Let freeze.

2. Cover a surface with newspaper to help avoid a mess.

3. Place the watercolor paper over the newspaper.

4. Use the watercolor ice cubes to paint! Make sure to wash your hands when you are done.

5. After you have finished, have an adult help you wash the ice cube tray thoroughly with hot water and soap. It is safe to use again.

OIL WATERCOLORS

3. Use more eyedroppers to drip a few colors of watercolor onto the paper. The colors should run, creating beautiful swirls.

4. Let dry overnight.

1. Gently dip your piece of paper into the tray of water. Remove it and place it in the empty tray.

2. Use an eyedropper to drip spots of oil onto the paper.

Delve to the Deep

Write a journal entry from the point of view of a deep-sea explorer who has discovered a brand-new animal species. Describe making your discovery, and then draw the animal and name it.

Now write a journal entry from the point of view of a deep-sea animal that encounters a deep-sea explorer. Think about how the animal feels about its new visitor, and describe what happens next!

_____

_____

_____

_____

_____

_____

_____

_____

_____

_____

_____

_____

_____

_____

_____

Turn an empty paper towel tube into a rocket.

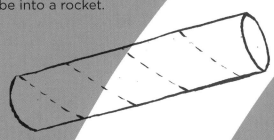

See if you can make a new dish using leftovers in your fridge.

Reuse a paper bag as the canvas for your next art piece.

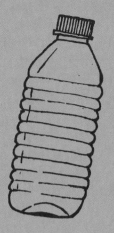

Decorate empty containers and use them to organize pens, pencils, and markers.

Create a portable game of tic-tac-toe for car rides. Make the pieces by writing *X* and *O* on plastic bottle caps with a permanent marker. Draw the game lines on a small cloth bag. Store the pieces in the bag.

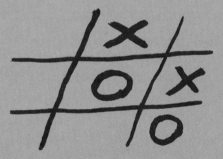

Turn a cardboard box into a "television" by having an adult help you cut a rectangular hole into one side. Use it to act out your own TV shows or movies.

Make Scrap Art

Instead of tossing the ends of veggies or your nut shells, why not turn them into cool art?

POTATO STAMPS

You Need

- A potato that is no longer good for eating, or a part of a potato that has been cut off because it has sprouted
- Knife
- Marker
- Water-based paint

1. If you have a whole potato, cut off one of the ends to use. Otherwise, use the piece that has been cut off already.

2. On the cut side, draw a simple shape, such as a star or a triangle.

3. Have an adult use the knife to carve around this shape, cutting back the rest of the potato piece so the shape sticks out.

4. Cover your shape in paint and get to stamping!

Tip! You can use the discarded tops of carrots as circle-shaped stamps.

SHELL BOATS

You Need

- Colorful Paper
- Scissors
- Glue
- Toothpicks
- Candle
- Match
- Walnut or pistachio shells

1. Have an adult help you cut a small piece of paper into the shape of a diamond about two inches tall and one inch wide at its widest point.

2. Fold the paper in half so that it becomes a triangle. Glue this piece around one end of a toothpick—this will be your flag.

3. Have an adult light your candle. After the wax starts to melt, the adult should pour some of this wax into a nut's shell, filling the shell about halfway.

4. Hold the bottom of the toothpick flag in the wax for about 30 seconds, or until it sets.

5. Test your boat! Does it float? Try making more boats and racing them.

Safety Tip!
Ask an adult for help with anything hot or sharp.

CITRUS GARLAND

You Need

- The peels of eaten citrus fruits, such as lemons, oranges, or grapefruits
- Small cookie cutters
- Scissors
- About 3 feet or more of string or twine

1. Use your small cookie cutters to cut out as many pieces from the peels as you can. If the cookie cutters won't cut all the way through the peels, have an adult help you cut out the shapes with scissors.

2. Use the scissors to poke a hole at the top of each shape.

3. Thread the string through your shapes. Separate the shapes along the string so they don't bunch together.

4. Spread each shape out on the garland. When you like how it looks, hang it. As the fruit dries, the shapes will shrink and give off a nice smell.

What other ways can you use scraps to make awesome art? You could try creating a sculpture out of those pistachio shells instead of boats, or you might try using an orange peel to make a bird feeder. Brainstorm some ideas here, and then try them out.

Craft New Things

Can you invent a new way to reuse? Pick an object from around your house that normally needs to be thrown out or recycled after it has been used. Come up with four different ways you could reuse this item and draw your ideas here. For example, could a tissue box become a toy car? Or could a detergent bottle be cleaned out and turned into a watering can?

1.

2.

3.

~~~~~~

4.

Bicycle Bonanza

Can you help repair this bicycle? Start at the top and head to the bottom, picking up the items listed below along the way.

Mr. Fix-it's Junk Shop

-HANDLE-BARS
-SEAT
-WHEEL
-FENDERS
-PEDALS
-CHAIN
-MIRROR
-HORN
-REFLECTOR
-FRAME

Start

Finish

Draw a house or bicycle made entirely of recycled and reused materials.

Reusing, Naturally!

This hermit crab is looking for a new, empty shell to use as its next home. Draw the crab the coolest or most beautiful shell you can come up with.

Swapping Shells

Unlike other types of crabs, hermit crabs do not grow hard, protective shells over their bodies. Instead, they find empty shells that are no longer being used by their former occupants. When a hermit grab outgrows its current shell, it leaves it and searches for a new one.

Think of wacky ways other animals in nature could reuse things fellow animals left behind. For example, what would it look like if a bird with a short tail collected discarded feathers to make a longer one? Draw your ideas here.

Grow New Food from Scraps

Cut down on food waste by using your scraps to create an indoor garden.

GROWING GREENS

You Need

- Scraps of leafy greens, such as lettuce, celery, fennel, cabbage, bok choy, scallions, or onions
- Shallow container
- Water
- Toothpicks (optional)

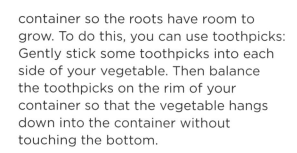

1. Start gathering your food scraps. The scraps are at the base of leafy greens (the part where the roots grow). Have an adult help you cut down the greens if needed. Make sure there is about one and a half inches of vegetable remaining above the base.

2. Fill your container with warm water.

3. Place the scraps into the container. For small vegetables, such as scallions, you can place several into one container. For larger vegetables, you may want to keep the base above the bottom of your container so the roots have room to grow. To do this, you can use toothpicks: Gently stick some toothpicks into each side of your vegetable. Then balance the toothpicks on the rim of your container so that the vegetable hangs down into the container without touching the bottom.

4. Wait and watch. Over time, the roots should grow and your scrap should begin to regrow its leafy green parts. You can harvest from this plant as it grows or replant it in a soil garden.

SCRAP LOG

Use this space to write a plant log. What do you notice about your scraps after one day? What about after one week?

Create Cutout Art

Draw a picture in this space. Then find some magazines or newspapers that are no longer being used. Re-create the picture you have drawn below on another piece of paper. Only this time, instead of drawing it, cut out images from the magazines or newspapers and glue them into a collage. See if you can find images that fit perfectly, or try combining parts of images to make a new object. (For example, you could cut out parts of different animals to make a brand-new animal.)

NnNnOooOPᵖP☮ᵒQᵃRᵣRᵣᵣSˢSˢSTᵢTTᵤUᵤUᵤVᵛVᵛWᵥWᵥWᵥXˣXˣxYᵧYᵧYZZᶻZZ

Make a recycled poem by cutting out the words you find in magazines and newspapers and arranging them onto a new piece of paper with glue. Let the words you find inspire your poem. Write a copy of it below.

ANSWER KEY

GROOVY MOVIES pg 16

PENGUIN PLAYTIME pg 32

COOL COMPETITIONS pg 40

SNOWY ADVENTURE pg 54

TOP SECRET MISSION pg 56

1. Crack the code. 2. Try it out. 3. Nice job.

DIVE IN pg 60

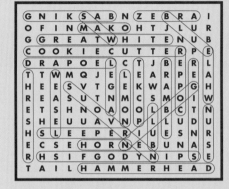

FISH SCHOOL pg 64

DOG DAZE pg 72

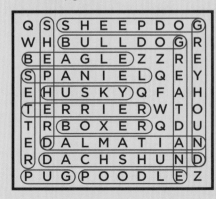

BOOK REVIEW pg 84

2. Leftover pizza, 3. Walking in the rain
4. Think before you speak, 5. Square dance,
6. Two wrongs don't make a right, 7. Half
past four, 8. Double vision, 9. Thundercloud

A-MAZE-ING MAZES pg 88

TRIVIA TIME pg 92

1. b; 2. c 3. c; 4. c; 5. True; 6. a; 7. c;
8. True; 9. c; 10. False

TUMMY TROUBLES pg 98

The fox ate too many DOUGHNUTS!

PARTY ON! pg 112

RAD ROBOTS pg 126

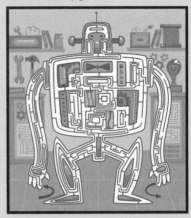

AMAZING INVENTIONS pg 137

BICYCLE BONANZA pg 150

CREDITS

Key: GI=Getty Images, IS= iStockphoto, SS=Shutterstock

Illustrations: Cover, 1, 4, 5, 10, 11, 25 (hands) 43, 45 (top, bottom) 62 (flower) 63 (note) 82 (list) 83 (pen) 85, 102 (dustpan, balls) 142 (roll) 143 (bottle, tictactoe) 158, 160 by Tom Jay; 12: LokFung/DigitalVision/GI; 16, 20 (clubhouse) 70, 90, 139 (canvas) by Mike Moran; 17: (tickets and clapper) Tetiana Lazunova/IS/GI, (film) Ruth J. Flanagan; 18, 44 (left) 102 (mail) by Sebastian Abboud, 22: (top) linearcurves/DigitalVision/GI; 22 (bottom) 27 by Jenny Campbell; 23: (bottom) Jolygon/IS/GI; 24: (ball) Carol Sutherby, (tictactoe) George Wildman, (hat) Brian White; 25: (letters) Viachaslau Vaitsenok/IS/GI; 25 (tiger) 62 (elephant) 63 (snail, whale) by neyro2008/IS/GI; 28: VeenaMari/DigitalVision/GI; 32: Dan McGeehan; 38 (coin) 51 (volcano) 53 (bottom) 56, 66 (snake) 104 (mail) 107 (top) 109 by Kelly Kennedy, 38: (wand) Nic Farrell; 39: Jason Tharp; 40: Barry Gott; 42: Andrew Brisman; 44: (right) primiaou/IS/GI; 45 (top) 122: (telescope) VeenaMari/ DigitalVision /GI; 46, 47: Vectorpower/IS/GI; 48: (center) Diane Palmisciano, (bottom) Rob McClurken; 52-53: gmm2000/ IS/GI; 53: (top) FrankRamspott/DigitalVision/GI; 54, 66 (flamingo) 82 (pineapple) by Neil Numberman; 55: (top) Karen Sneide, (bottom) Keith Frawley; 57: (stamp) Zdenek Bohm/Alamy; 60 (starfish) 100 (starfish) by Dave Joly; 60: (crossword) Marta Ruliffson; 61 (shells) 66 (dog) 92 (diamond) by David Coulson; 61: (jelly) Michaela Schuett; 63: (window) ourlifelooklikeballoon/IS/GI, (butterfly) Tim Davis; 64, 67 by Erica Sirotich; 66: (bottom) Deb Melmon; 71, 100 (butterfly) by Claudine Gevry; 72, 92 by Jack Desrocher; 74: Berta Maluenda; 77 Dan Sipple; 82: (triangle) Nattiya Ruankum/IS/GI; 83: (envelope) studiogstock/IS/GI; 86: (poodle) Bob Ostrum, (bear) Rico Schacherl; 86 (snake) 110 (broom) Mike Dammer; 88: Pixelboy Studio; 91: (border) CSA-Archive/DigitalVision/GI, (toy) Marisa Morea, (dog) Katie McDee; 92: (otters) Dana Regan, (firework) drogatnev/IS/GI, (mummy) James Loram, (bolt) Sudowoodo/IS/GI; 94-95: (top) Jason Thorne; 94-95 (line art) 122 (alien) by Ron Zalme; 98: (puzzle) Jennifer Harney; 100: (spider) Alton Langford, (book) Julissa Mora, (turtle) Patrick Girouard, (worm) Joey Ellis; 101, 111, 120 (cart) 138 (bottom) by Kevin Zimmer; 103: (hearts) Dimitris Stephanides/DigitalVision/GI, (earth) Olga Prokopeva/IS/GI, (mirror) Rocky Fuller; 106: (emoji) Pingebat/IS/GI; 107: (bottom) Jane Sanders; 108: (border) Janee Trasler, (calendar) Aleksandra Alekseeva/IS/GI; 112: Julissa Mora; 114: (camera) vitalkaka/IS/GI; 116-117: Iuliia Alysheva/IS/GI; 117: Holli Conger; 119: Mariia Arsonova/IS/GI; 122 (planets) 125 by Mike Lowery, 122: (test tube) Elizabeth Allyn Hendricks; 123: (robot) topform84/IS/GI (clock) Christine Schneider; 126: Tom Woolley; 128: (alien) Jo Moon; 128-129: (background) orensila/IS/GI; 130, 148 (box) by Rita Lascaro; 132-133: (top) Ruth Flanigan; 135 Hayelin Choi; 137: Jackie Stafford; 139 (splash) wattanaphob/IS/GI; 140: (reef) Tim Budgen; 141: Erin Mauterer; 142: (food) Tom Bingham, (bag) Joyce Haynes; 143: (bag) Sean Parkes; 150: Judith Hunt; 151: (bike) Mike Boley. Photos: 6, 7: Annette Kiesow; 8-9: (corners) LiliGraphie/Alamy; 9: (magazines) OxanaD/IS/GI, (ribbon) FabrikaCr/ IS/GI, (sticks) 9, 80 (doghouse) 89, 106 (sponges) 115, 124 (eyes) 132, 149 (bowling) by Guy Cali Associates, Inc., 8: (cup) malerapaso/IS/GI, (envelope) pics five/SS; 14: unalozmen/IS/GI; 15: (candy) karandaev/IS/GI, (marshmallow) heinteh/IS/GI; 17 (popcorn) Thatphichai Yodsri/IS/GI; 19: (sports) JulNichols/ IS/GI, (palette) artisteer/IS/GI, (game pieces) jsolie/E+/GI; 20: (books) Elnur/IS/GI; 21: Floortje/E+/GI; 23: (top) Prostock-Studio/IS/GI; 29 (top) Michael Burrell/ IS/GI, (bottom) laurien/E+/GI; 30: Worawut Prasuwan/IS/GI; 33: JamesMDrakeMedia/IS/GI; 34-35: ihsanyildizli/ IS/GI; 36: (jacks) jkennedy561/IS/GI, (dice) SteveGreen1953/IS/GI; 37: Robert Koopmans/E+/GI; 38: (pencil) Boris Yankov/E+/GI, (banana) EVAfotografie/IS/GI, (soccer) irni Torfason/IS/GI, (trebuchet) ZargonDesign/IS/ GI, (pumpkin) MariuszBlach/IS/GI, (guitar) gradyreese/IS/GI; 48 (top) Africa Studio/SS; 50: Vershinin-M/ IS/GI; 51: (gummies) Floortje/IS/GI; 57: (paper) Michael Burrell/Alamy; 58: (lime) rimglow/IS/GI, (lemon) Kelenart/IS/GI; 59: natrot/ IS/GI; 60 (shark) Hemera Technologies/Jupiter Images; 65: (top) burnsboxco/IS/GI, (background) Maya Parfentieva/IS/ GI; 68: (top) Olesya Eroshenko/IS/GI; 69: thousandlies/IS/GI; 73, 76 (squirrel, cow, kangaroo) 98 (fox) 153 by GlobalP/IS/ GI; 76: (dolphin) bbevren/IS/GI, (scorpion) andrewburgess/IS/GI, Martin J Calabrese/IS/GI; 78: J33P3l2/IS/GI; 79: (dog) Baramyou0708/IS/GI, (treats) matt_benoit/IS/GI; 80: (bulldog) WilleeCole/IS/GI, (puppy) Dorottya_Mathe/IS/GI; 87: Alexandra Surkova/IS/GI; 90: (top) Serg_Velusceac/IS/GI; 91: Mariia Demchenko/IS/GI; 92: (cat) PavelHlystov/IS/GI; 99, 149 (tissues) by subjug/IS/GI; 100: (Saturn) dottedhippo/IS/GI, (flower) VIDOK/E+/GI; 104 (bin) ranplett/E+/GI; 105, 155 by stockcam/E+/GI 106: (cookies) YinYang/E+/GI, (envelope) Photoevent/E+/GI; 110: (laundry, clutter) urfinguss/IS/GI, (list) Ralf Geithe/IS/GI; 112: (top) kyoshino/IS/GI; 113: mphillips007/IS/GI; 114: (block) Yevhenii Orlov/IS/GI, (shell) kyoshino/IS/GI, (buttons) Almaje/IS/GI; 118-119: Jiri Hera/Alamy; 118: domin_domin/E+/GI; 120: (background) Rockard/IS/ GI, (fork) Meliha Gojak/IS/GI, 124-125 (teeth) Anton Novikov/IS/GI; 124: foto-ruhrgebiet/IS/GI, (orange slime) Toxitz/ IS/GI; 127: ThomasVogel/IS/GI; 135: (coins) eldadcarin/IS/GI, (lemon) Su Nitram/IS/GI; 136: moonisblack/IS/GI; 138: (top) Hubble/ESA/NASA/CFHT/NOAO; 139: (bottles) sunstock/IS/GI, (ice tray) wattanaphob/IS/GI; 140 (notebook) hudiemm/ E+/GI; 144: Alas_spb/IS/GI; 145: karayuschij/IS/GI; 146: (top) TatianaMara/Shutterstock, (center) ivanmateev/IS/GI, (bottom) 13-Smile/IS/GI; 147: cisilya/IS/GI; 148: (bottom) 151: (background) deskoul/IS/GI; 152: busypix/IS/GI; 154: tookitook/IS/GI; 156-157: (top) Wylius/IS/GI, 156: (bottom) Thinglass/IS/GI; 157: (magazines) Franz-W. Franzelin/E+/GI.

Published by Highlights Press
815 Church Street
Honesdale, Pennsylvania 18431
ISBN: 978-1-64472-943-4
Manufactured in Dongguan, Guangdong, China
Mfg. 08/2022

First edition
Visit our website at Highlights.com.
10 9 8 7 6 5 4 3 2 1

Produced by WonderLab Group, LLC
Writer: Paige Towler
Designer: Nicole Lazarus ·
Photo Editor: Annette Kiesow
Copy Editor: Molly Reid
Proofreader: Susan Hom